The Splendour of

WINDSOR

ETON, HAMPTON COURT AND LEGOLAND

160 COLOUR ILLUSTRATIONS - 11 MAPS

Victoria Memorial and Windsor Castle.

Cover:
Windsor's Castle. Air View.

(P. 2/3) Windsor's Castle. Air View.

THOMAS BENACCI LTD
LONDON

St. George's Chapel. Main entrance.

Guildhall.

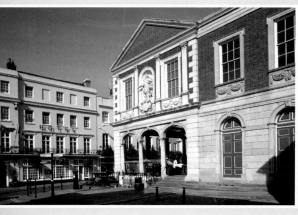

Long Walk.

Legoland. Tower Bridge.

Hampton Court Palace. South Facade.

Eton College.

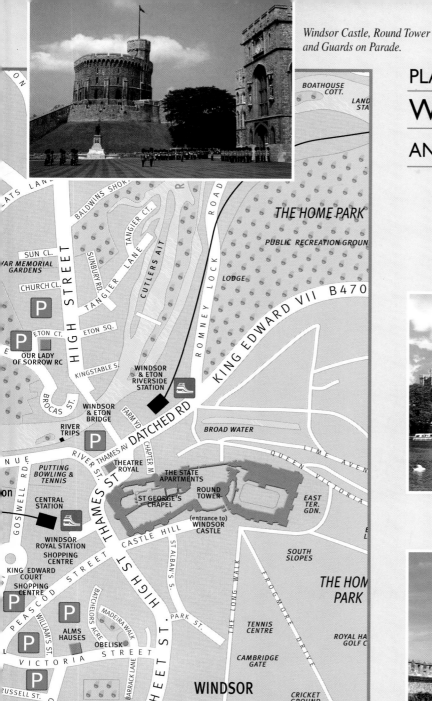

Windsor Castle, Round Tower and Guards on Parade.

PLAN OF
WINDSOR
AND ETON

THE HOME PARK

PUBLIC RECREATION GROUN

BOATHOUSE COTT.

LAND STA

KING EDWARD VII B470

ROMNEY LOCK ROAD

LODGE

BALDWINS SHOR

BALDWINS SHORE

TANGIER CT.

TANGIER LANE

CUTLERS AIT

SUNBURY RD.

HIGH STREET

SUN CL.

WAR MEMORIAL GARDENS

CHURCH CL.

ETON CT.

ETON SQ.

OUR LADY OF SORROW RC

KINGSTABLE S.

KINGSTABLE S.

BROCAS ST.

WINDSOR & ETON BRIDGE

RIVER TRIPS

FARM YD

DATCHED RD

CHAPTER M

WINDSOR & ETON RIVERSIDE STATION

BROAD WATER

LIME AVEN

QUEEN VICTORIA

Round Tower on William I's Motte viewed from river.

RIVER ST.

THAMES AV

THAMES ST

HIGH ST

GOSWELL RD.

PUTTING BOWLING & TENNIS

THEATRE ROYAL

CENTRAL STATION

WINDSOR ROYAL STATION

SHOPPING CENTRE

KING EDWARD COURT

SHOPPING CENTRE

PEASCOD STREET

WILLIAM'S ST.

ALMS HAUSES

MADEIRA WALK

BATCHELORS ACRE

OBELISK

VICTORIA STREET

RUSSELL ST.

ROAD

ALBANY RD.

DAGMAR R.

KEPPEL ST.

VICTORIA BARRACKS

BARRACK LANE

SHEET ST.

BROOK ST.

K CL.

THE STATE APARTMENTS

ST GEORGE'S CHAPEL

ROUND TOWER

(entrance to) WINDSOR CASTLE

CASTLE HILL

ST ALBAN'S S.

PARK ST.

THE LONG WALK

EAST TER. GDN.

SOUTH SLOPES

THE HOME PARK

FROGMORE DRIVE

WALK

TENNIS CENTRE

CAMBRIDGE GATE

ROYAL HA GOLF C

CRICKET GROUND

FROGMORE

QUEE

BORDER

WINDSOR

Windsor Castle.

Hampton Court Palace.

TOWN WALKABOUT

Edward IV's reconstruction of Windsor Castle in the C15th, notably St George's Chapel, brought new life to the town. In Elizabethan times the air in Windsor was considered to be the sweetest and purest within 30 miles of London.

Enter Church Street, the scene of C16th poetic inspiration and C17th royal passions. William Shakespeare is said to have written the 'Merry Wives of Windsor' in the Old King's Head. King Charles II is reputed to have purchased *Drury House* and nearby *Burford House* for the use and abode of his favourite mistress Nell Gwynn. A tunnel then conveniently connected the former with the Castle.

Why not indulge your own passion, of a culinary nature, by sampling sumptuous fare in one of the quaint and reputedly haunted restaurants.

Turn the corner into Church Lane and evoke the past through your fingertips in the brass-rubbing centre, annexed to the Church of St John the Baptist built in 1820. Above the connecting passage a plaque commemorates the early C19th Engine House which stored the parish fire engine.

Church Street, Flower Seller.

Church Street. The house used by King Charles II.

Guildhall.

Market Cross house.

The impressive Guildhall, designed by Sir Thomas Fitch and built in 1687-89, invites closer inspection: Sir Christopher Wren, in defiance of Council sceptics, built the columns short of the ceiling of the Council chamber. No longer a Corn Exchange, the open area is frequently used to market high quality crafts. Leaning precariously towards the Guildhall is **Market Cross House**, dating from around 1687 and once connected by a tunnel to the Castle. Adjacent Queen Charlotte Street is the shortest street in England and only a few strides away from the former medieval market area of the town.

St. John the Baptist Church.

Victoria Memorial and Windsor Castle.

Opposite, the Royal Windsor Information Centre houses the Town and Crown Exhibition. Queen Victoria's statue points the way with her sceptre towards **Peascod Street** which, in medieval times, was the route to the Royal Hunting Lodge.

Shops in Peascod Street.

Curfew Tower. Windsor Castle Wall, West Side .

In **Curfew Yard**, in 1648, Oliver Cromwell (later Lord Protector of England) was said to have signed the death warrant of Charles I. A blocked tunnel leads from the basement to the dungeons in the Curfew Tower.

ENTERTAINMENT

Church Street.

Thames Street, Edward VIII's Boots Passage.

Sir Christopher Wren's House.

Windsor Thames Street.

White Hart Hotel.

Guarded by a bust of King Edward VIII, Boots Passage displays a tiled aerial view of Windsor Castle based on an engraving by Wenceslaus Hollar in 1663. Beyond lies Alexandra Gardens, coach park and river. Why not sojourn the night or for refreshments at **Sir Christopher Wren's House**, built by the famous architect as his family home in 1676.

Pamper yourself - wine and dine in one of Windsor's historic hotels or chic restaurants.

Indulge your fancy - purchase that special gift from quaint Church Street or from Thames Street, site of King George III's original Theatre Royal.

*Prince Charles
playing polo
on Smiths' Lawn.*

Cruising on the river.

Windsor Horse Show at night.

Regimental Band.

Round Tower on William I's Motte viewed from river.

RIVER THAMES

Cruises may be arranged which connect with Hampton Court Palace and Runnimede, site of the historic signing of the Magna Carta in 1215.

In the reign of Henry III, water from the river, 164 feet below the present day Castle, was drawn into a well in the Round Tower possibly as a precaution in times of siege. In the more settled early C19th an ice carnival took place on the frozen river.

In contrast, in 1852, the aptly named Thames St. was flooded, impeding access to the castle.

Looking across to Eton.

Riverside restaurant.

Ready for a cruise.

Boats for hire.

THE LONG WALK AND COPPER HORSE

Discover the sensory pleasure of more than 5000 acres of great Parkland, perhaps first glimpsed from the Long Walk. The prestigious 3-mile (4.5km) long treelined avenue was laid out in the reign of Charles II. Oak largely replaced original elms in Victorian times while the existing beech trees replaced diseased stock in 1942.

Unaltered by the passage of time or fashion, the Romanesque equestrian statue of King George III commands an elevated position at

'Copper Horse'.
King George III statue.

the end of the Long Walk on Snow Hill. George IV's memorial to his father stands 50' (15m) high from its base, the horse being large enough to accommodate sixteen people. Since the inauguration of the Ascot races by Queen Anne in 1711, horses and carriages have reverberated in royal procession down the Long Walk. Queen Victoria took the same route from Windsor Castle to her final resting-place at Frogmore.

On a merrier note, on 19th June 1999 a journey of love and devotion carried the bride Sophie Rhys-Jones and her groom HRH Prince Edward towards the Castle. Never before had a royal wedding car been decorated with a white bridal ribbon.

Windsor Castle. The Long Walk.

Windsor Castle. Round Tower with standard flying.

WINDSOR CASTLE

Windsor Castle Regimental Band.

In this new millenium Windsor Castle stands unchallenged as the largest continuously occupied castle in the world. The Castle is perched on an elongated chalk escarpment 100 feet above the River Thames. Now boasting more than 5000 acres of parkland, the royal domain once encompassed the vast Windsor Great Forest where the Normans introduced deer parks and Henry VIII enjoyed hawking and hunting wild boar and the noble stag.

During more than 900 years successive monarchs have imprinted their character upon the Castle.

William I's construction of an earthen mound or motte in the Middle Ward, housing the keep, was used by Henry II to support his Round Tower in stone. The original motte remains, the Tower being heightened and embellished for the sake of prestige in the reign of King George IV.

Windsor Castle. Curtain Wall guarding Round Tower.

Upper Ward with State and Private Apartments and Statue of Charles II.

Windsor Castle. Round Tower and Guards.

Windsor Castle, Guardsman at front of State Apartments.

Windsor Castle, King Henry VIII Gate and Towers.

Windsor Castle, Saxon and Round Towers.

P. 17. Windsor Castle, 'Norman' Gate and Motte Garden.

PLAN OF
THE CASTLE

Round Tower.

St George's Chapel.

Henry VIII Gate.

Military Knights' Lodgings.

'Norman Gate'.

The Quadrangle and the statue of Charles II.

St. George's Gate.

William 'The Conqueror'.

'A man of great wisdom and power'
He was described as 'that stark man'
Fortifications were erected in a ring around London,
and in Windsor an earthen Motte with wooden towers.

WILLIAM THE 'CONQUEROR'

(1066 - 1087) - (Plantagenet)

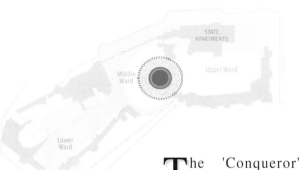

Windsor Castle, Round Tower.

The 'Conqueror' defeated King Harold II at the Battle of Hastings in 1066, as depicted in the Bayeux Tapestry. In 1086 he ordered the 'Domesday Survey' representing the largest collection of data in Europe relating to population, land and livestock ownership in order to maximize tax revenues.

A tall, clean-shaven man, possibly of Nordic descent, William was described by his subjects as 'that stark man': the punishment for killing a stag was to suffer blinding.

William and his wife Mathilde appear to have been devoted and faithful companions.

King William's overriding concern was to consolidate his new conquest by erecting fortifications in a ring around London, within one day's march of the capital.

Windsor's chalk escarpment, rising 100 feet above the River Thames, was leased for 12 shillings a year and a new fortress of wood was built there upon a motte or artificial mound of earth.

Windsor Great Park was restocked with rabbit warrens and hares while deer were introduced to satisfy the Norman love of hunting.

Oak trees were planted as part of a new forest management to replenish wood reserves for vital construction.

Windsor Great Forest.

Windsor Castle, Round Tower and Guards on Parade.

Henry II.

*Curtain wall, Round Tower and castle
were rebuilt mainly in stone
Nineteen watchtowers were erected.*

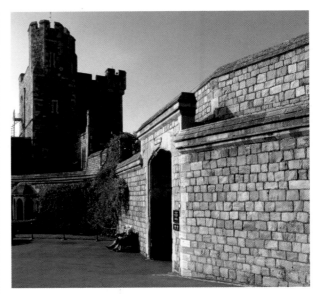

Windsor Castle. Winchester Tower.

HENRY II

(1154 - 1189)

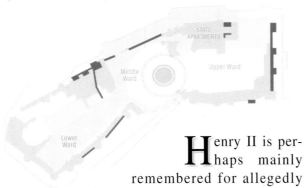

Henry II is perhaps mainly remembered for allegedly ordering the murder of his Chancellor, Thomas Beckett, on the matter of the Church's jurisdiction over the Courts. The King's fourth and favourite son John, later King John, was responsible for sealing the Magna Carta in 1215.

Windsor Castle. Curfew Tower and Castle Wall, overlooking Thames Street.

Windsor Castle's ephemeral wooden structure was rebuilt in stone, using massive boulders of resiliant heathstone dragged for miles across the former Great Windsor Forest. Prisoners held in the Curfew Tower were able to scoop out the soft chalk infilling until the very thickness of the walls defeated them.

Windsor Castle was then arranged into three baileys or Wards. Thirty feet lower than its later modified form, the Round Tower served its purpose as a keep or stronghold. A half mile long Curtain wall in stone took sixty years to complete and defended the Lower Ward. The north side of the Upper Ward, the steepest side facing the river, continued to be reserved for the family's own occupation.

Nineteen watchtowers were erected during the troublesome closing years of the monarch's reign.

Henry III.

Added 5 rounded towers in stone to Curtain wall.
Royal Chapel built on the site of Albert Memorial Chapel,
Lower Ward.

HENRY III

(1216 - 1272)

Rounded tower in Curtain Wall, Thames Street.

Only nine years old when he acceded to the throne, Henry III was the son of King John who, in 1215, had sealed the Magna Carta. He became a great patron of ecclesiastical architecture and undertook the rebuilding of Westminster Abbey. Windsor Castle was a favoured residence, his Queen Eleanor and many of their six children sojourning here for long periods. One of their daughters, Margaret, was born at the Castle.

At Windsor Castle cisterns were constructed to collect clean rain water, a well in the Round Tower connecting with the River Thames. The Castle's defences were strengthened, the west wall being repaired in stone.

Following the two sieges in connection with the feud between Henry II's sons Richard and John, five rounded

Windsor Castle, Round Tower with battlements.

towers were added in stone to the Curtain wall. The round design adopted by Richard I was less vulnerable to attack than the traditional English square structure. Queen Eleanor's comfort was improved by the addition of even more luxurious apartments in the Upper Ward, "contiguous with the King's, and under the same roof".

In the Lower Ward the Royal Chapel dedicated to Edward the Confessor, was built between 1240-1248, and occupied the site of the present Albert Memorial Chapel.

Edward III.

The king expanded the building at the castle.
In the Upper Ward a Gothic Palace was arranged.
A new St George's Hall was erected.
The 'Norman Gate' separated the Upper and Lower Wards.

EDWARD III

(1327 - 1377)

Procession of the Noble Order of the Garter.

His claim to Philip VI's throne of France began the so-called Hundred Years War. Edward's reign witnessed both the ravages of the Black Death and the early masterpieces of Chaucer. Possibly influenced by the romantic Legend of King Arthur and the Knights of the Round Table, Edward created the Order of the Garter, the most Noble Order of Chivalry in Europe.

Prince Edward was born at Windsor Castle and was baptized in the old Chapel of St Edward. Following the death of his Queen, Philippa of Hainaut, the King became a virtual recluse at Windsor. In stature Edward was described as tall and of impressive build. A skilled warrior, his physical attributes seem to have contributed toward his triumph at the battle of Crécy in 1346.

Edward III founded the College of St George and the Order of the Garter at Windsor in 1348. Twenty-six Poor Knights served to pray for king and country on behalf of the Knights of the Garter. Every year on St George's Day a ceremonial banquet took place using the old St George's Hall.

Each June the present Monarch dons a cloak of dark blue velvet, the blue garter holding the emblem of the Garter Star: 'Honi soit qui mal y pense' (shame on him who thinks evil of it).

In 1348, work was begun at the Castle. King David of Scotland was ransomed for 100,000 crowns to help finance construction.

The Chapel of Edward the Confessor was extensively altered and dedicated to St George. The misnamed 'Norman Gate', with its own portcullis, separated the Upper and Lower Wards. Edward favoured impressive Gothic architecture of pointed arches and flying buttresses, a style which had been introduced by Henry III. In 1357 the Bishop of Winchester, William of Wykeham, was instructed to direct the construction of the Upper Ward. The outcome was a large Gothic Palace arranged around inner courtyards. A new St George's Hall with an impressive arched-beam ceiling was erected between 1362-5, to house banquets for Knights of the Garter.

Windsor Castle,
'Norman Gate'.

Edward IV.

War of the Roses: more than 36,000 men
were slain in one day.
Building of St George's Chapel,
and New Cloisters.

EDWARD IV

(1461 - 1483)

E dward was declared King by Parliament in 1461 after defeating the Lancastrians during the war of the Roses in the bloodiest battle ever on British soil, when more than 36,000 men were slain in one day. He was deposed in 1470 and restored to the throne less than one year later.

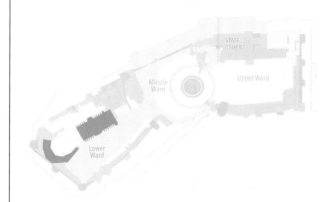

Windsor Castle, St George's Chapel.

Windsor Castle, Dean's Cloister.

His greatest memorial is St George's Chapel, Windsor Castle, home of the ancient Chivalrous Order of the Garter.

King Edward was reported to have had the physique of a warrior and the propensity to be pleasure seeking. He was tall and burly, his lead coffin measuring 6'3" in length. Talents included the military art, and dancing, both of which seemed to have endeared him to the ladies. He married rather furtively in 1464 the beautiful and widowed Lady Grey (née Elizabeth Woodville) who bore him 10 children.

Edward's marriage alienated influential followers, the Civil War was reopened and the King was forced for a period to flee to France.

Solar Clock, St. George's Chapel.

Whilst at Windsor, the King enjoyed impressing his guests. During a reception given in honour of Lord Grutheryse, Edward presented the ambassador with a cup of gold, inlaid with pearls and sapphires. The following day's itinerary included hunting, followed by a tour of the Castle gardens and Vineyard. Evensong preceded a banquet given by the Queen at 9.00 p.m. after which a tour of the royal apartments feasted the eye. After bathing, the guest was treated to 'green ginger, divers syrups, sweets and spicy wine'.

A new St George's Chapel was created, the finest building in the whole Castle compound. The founder is buried here, beneath a simple black stone, in the vicinity of the Cloisters for which he was also responsible.

ST GEORGE'S CHAPEL

St George's Chapel has been described as 'the shrine of British royalty'. Ten English Monarchs are buried here and six Queens. Here lies Henry VIII who requested to be buried in the same vault as his favourite Queen Consort, Jane Seymour. Sixteen Yeomen of the Guard of exceptional height and strength carried his massive lead coffin. The widowed Catherine Parr, Henry VIII's sixth and last wife, observed the funeral from the Queen's closet, originally designed for the first Queen Consort Catherine of Aragon. Her own emblem of pomegranates can be seen among the awe-inspiring ornamentation.

Shortly before his execution Charles I spent his last Christmas at Windsor Castle, as a prisoner. His burial was conducted in silence and without the usual pomp and ceremony on the orders of Oliver Cromwell, Lord Protector of the newly found government during the Interregnum (1649-1658). Even the location of King Charles I's tomb remained secret until 1813 when the Prince Regent (later George IV) decided to settle the issue. Where do you think he was interred? A clue may be provided by a particular stone slab on the floor of the Chapel Choir wherein lies the vault of Henry VIII.

Windsor Castle, St George's Chapel, stone sculpture.

Windsor Castle,
St George's Chapel,
detail of King's Beasts.

Windsor Castle, Cloister and St George's Chapel.

Windsor Castle, King's beasts stand guard above St George's Chapel.

Windsor Castle. St George's Chapel, detail of heraldic coat-of-arms.
(P. 30-31) St George's Chapel. The choir stalls.

St George's Chapel has witnessed several royal weddings. When Queen Victoria's eldest son and heir, HRH Albert Edward, the Prince of Wales, was married to Alexandra of Denmark on 10th March 1863, she secluded herself from the scrutiny of the public in the Queen's Closet. Only one year and three months previously she had herself lost, through bereavement, her own beloved partner in marriage, her Consort Prince Albert. On the day of his engagement to Miss Sophie Rhys Jones, Prince Edward had described the Chapel as "a glorious piece of architecture" in "a wonderful setting".

A masterpiece of medieval perpendicular architecture the Chapel was built as a spiritual home for the Order of the Garter. Construction began in 1475 in the reign of Edward IV but was not completed until 50 years later in the reign of Henry VIII. The Chapel's name was inspired by King Edward III' s enchantment with the legends of King Arthur and the Knights of the Round Table.

Every June the reigning monarch presides over the ceremony of the Order of the Garter, seated in an elaborately carved stall, accompanied by a fanfare of trumpets, anthems and prayers and the uplifting music of the great organ. During the Garter Ceremony in 1666 Samuel Pepys described the Chapel as "a noble place indeed". Glance upwards and capture the multi-coloured splendour of heraldic banners, crowned by the intricately carved fan-vaulted roof completed in 1528. Consider the C15th stalls in the Choir, with their boldly expressed heraldic art, displaying each Knight's coat-of-arms, crest, mantle and helm (witnessed overleaf).

Windsor Castle, King's Beast on top of St George's Chapel.

Henry VIII.

Henry VIII Gateway, Lower Ward.
He had six wives: Catherine of Aragon, Anne Boleyn
Jane Seymour, Anne of Cleves, Catherine Howard, Catherine Parr.

HENRY VIII

(1509 - 1547)

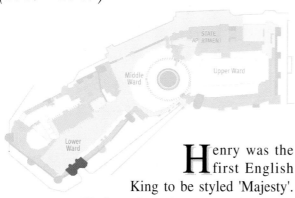

Henry was the first English King to be styled 'Majesty'. He is perhaps best remembered for having had six wives, two of whom were beheaded. He met Anne Boleyn at Windsor Castle. Henry held the balance of power in Europe, defied the papacy in Rome, was responsible for the dissolution of monasteries in England, and in 1534, appointed himself the supreme Head of the Church. He was the founder of Trinity College, Cambridge. Henry fathered Mary (later Mary I) and Elizabeth (later Elizabeth I).

Henry VIII is the most famous English King. As a young man he was regarded as the most accomplished prince of his age - handsome, athletic, a skilled hunter, capable musician and linguist. His prowess at jousting, including at Windsor, earned him the nickname 'Bluff King Hal'. Here he often did "....Ride forth on hawking or walks in the Park". His hunting sword is on display in the Queen's Chamber at Windsor Castle.

Round Tower and Garden.

Perhaps his courtship of Anne Boleyn took place within view of the Round Tower. The King's person would be instantly recognized on arrival at the castle by his large square face, red-gold beard and familiar slash and bejewelled attire. When the ageing Henry chose the spirited Duchess of Milan for his fourth wife she was said to have not only refused his suit, but remarked had she two heads the King of England might be welcome to one of them - halas, she had only one.

Shortly after his marriage, in 1509, to Catherine of Aragon, Henry left his palace at Greenwich and brought the entire court to Windsor Castle. Here Garter ceremonies were lavish. Within the first

36 | *** Henry ordered the construction of gateway to the Lower Ward. King gateway comprises a wide arch supeither side by massive stone towers. the archway bears the King's symbols of lis, fleur-de-lis and the combined roses of aster and Yorkshire, do you know the purpose the holes in the stonework? Had you been an unwelcome visitor to Henry's court, you may have

been anointed with boiling oil. The King is said to have been responsible for developing the North Terrace, now obscured by trees, which provided a panoramic view of the Thames Valley.

At Windsor Castle Henry met his second wife, Anne Boleyn, whom he espied sewing in Canon's Cloisters in the Lower Ward. Perhaps her reputedly fine eyes and youth, persuaded the King to divorce Catherine of Aragon who had, in six years of marriage, failed to bear him any living sons and heirs. When the Pope refused to grant permission for Henry to annul his first marriage, the King responded by declaring himself supreme Head of

Henry VIII Gateway.

Madame Tussaud's. Henry VIII and his six wives.

Round Tower on William I's Motte viewed from the same river that transported King Henry VIII from London.

the Church. Not only were the monasteries investigated and purged of abbots and monks, at Windsor a local popular preacher Anthony Pearson was burnt at the stake in a meadow north of the Castle.

The moment Henry heard the guns at the Tower announcing Anne's death he joined Jane Seymour, was formally betrothed the next day and married ten days later. Imagine Henry's delight when Jane produced a much longed for though sickly son and heir (later King Edward VI) and his despair when the Queen died twelve days later. Princess Mary was requested to assume the chief mourner's role at the funeral which was held at Windsor Castle.

The young King Edward VI was reputed to find the Castle cold and less comfortable than Hampton Court Palace. Henry's fourth marriage to Anne of Cleves was solemnized on 6th January 1540. Perhaps the shortest lived alliance was his marriage to Anne, which lasted only six months.

Catherine Howard, Henry's fifth wife, was reputed to be sensual and beguiling yet due to her infidelity was beheaded less than two years later.

Henry's sixth and final wife, Catherine Parr, observed his funeral from the Queen's closet, St George's Chapel.

Henry VIII died at Whitehall in London in 1547 and was buried at Windsor. When the cortege reached Henry VIII's Gateway to the Castle, the procession stretched for more than three miles from Windsor's bridge.

Mary I (Bloody Mary).

Mary Tudor Tower
Construction of Military Knights Houses in Lower Ward.

QUEEN MARY I

(1553 - 1558)

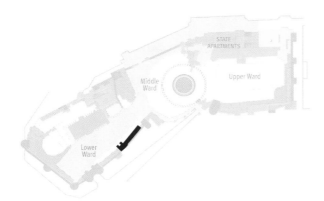

Mary Tudor Tower.

An ardent Catholic, Mary's attempts to eradicate Protestantism, including the execution of Thomas Cranmer, Archbishop of Canterbury, earned her the nickname 'Bloody Mary'. Her marriage alliance with Spain threatened the sovereignty of England and culminated in the loss of Calais, the last remaining Continental possession.

Mary, though in poor health, was the only child to survive infancy of the union between King Henry VIII and his first wife Catherine of Aragon.

Born a congenital syphilitic, Mary endured chronic ill health, including headaches, poor eyesight and ulcerative rhinitis. The disease is believed to have been passed on by her mother who contracted it from her first husband Arthur, elder brother of King Henry.

Mary's relationship with her father was erratic. Initially considered a disappointment because of her gender, she was later given her own court.

Queen Mary honoured the terms of Henry VIII's will by constructing military Knights' lodgings in the Lower Ward at Windsor Castle. Poor Knights who had distinguished themselves as soldiers were recompensed with well-maintained accommodation.

Perhaps the greatest sadness in Mary's life was the failure of her marriage in 1554 to the Catholic Philip II of Spain. In lasting memory of their short union, the C14th belfry at Windsor Castle became Mary Tudor Tower and bears both her arms and those of her husband, King Philip II of Spain.

"When I am dead", Mary had said, "you will find the words 'Philip' and 'Calais' engraved upon my heart".

Mary Tudor Tower and Military Knights' Lodgings.

Elizabeth I.

Queen Elizabeth Terrace.
Addition of Long Gallery, now Royal Library.

ELIZABETH I

(1558 - 1603)

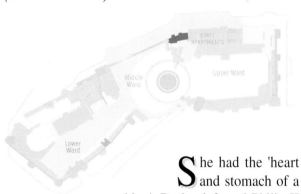

North Terrace Entrance.

North Terrace (Queen Elizabeth I Terrace) and 'Norman Gate'.

S he had the 'heart and stomach of a king'. Drake defeated Philip II of Spain's Armada in 1588. The American Colony of Virginia is named after the 'Virgin Queen' who never married.

Daughter of Anne Boleyn, Elizabeth was Henry VIII's strongest and healthiest child. She was said to read "now at Windsor more Greek every day than some Prebendary of this church doth read Latin in a whole week".

Dubbed 'Gloriana', Elizabeth's attire was magnificent, bejewelled and adorned with her favourite pearls against a glorious halo of red hair.

Her love of riches extended to adorning the royal beds at Windsor Castle with bed hangings and tapestries of gold and fine silk. Talented at needlework, one state visitor to the Castle enthused about a "beautifully embroidered cushion done by Queen Elizabeth herself in red and white silk".

"Although the house be cold", Windsor Castle became the winter retreat of the Queen in 1563, following the outbreak of plague in London. Here she bathed in rooms "ceiled and wainscoted with looking glass".

Warmed by great fires and entertained by gathering around her children who enacted plays, Queen Elizabeth's fondness for the theatre lead to her commissioning the revered bard William Shakespeare to write "The Merry Wives of Windsor". Shakespeare is reputed to have written the play in the King's Head, now a restaurant.

The Queen walked in the gardens, usually for an hour every day before dinner. In 1572 Elizabeth ordered the restoration of her much-loved terrace.

In 1580 Elizabeth added the Long Gallery to the State Apartments (now the Royal Library).

Charles I.

Oliver Cromwell's resolution:"The King should be prosecuted for his life as a criminal person". Charles I was buried at Windsor after execution at Whitehall.

CHARLES I

(1625 - 1649)

Referred to as the 'Martyr King', Charles was the only English monarch to be beheaded. His execution at Whitehall in London, 1649, signalled the end of monarchical rule for 51 years. King Charles I's last word on the scaffold was "Remember".

During the first summer of the king's reign, when there was an outbreak of plague, the gates of Windsor Castle were locked and the royal party departed. In 1635 by a decree of court "dust and other rubbish" was removed from the unsavoury streets of Windsor. New wells were dug in the vicinity of Market Cross House in 1637.

Charles I adopted his father's belief in 'the divine right of kings'. Three times he summoned Parliament which he then dissolved.

When the king's attempt to arrest five troublesome members of Parliament in January 1642 failed, he removed his family, troops and ammunition to Windsor.

Today enjoy the ceremonial parade of guards, in contrast to the military guards who held Charles I captive.

The Walls that imprisoned Charles I.

Final resting place of King Charles I.

Curfew Yard provided the setting of the fateful resolution proclaimed by Oliver Cromwell that "the King should be prosecuted for his life as a criminal person". King Charles I was accused of high treason in 1648.

He spent his last Christmas at Windsor Castle. Although he was not permitted the customary fare of mince pies and plum porridge, he could "walk where and when he pleased" and sleep in his own bed-chamber.

King Charles I's final visit to Windsor Castle was in a coffin draped with a black velvet pall. When a sudden snowstorm turned the pall white some said that Heaven had declared the King's innocence.

Charles II.

*He transformed the Upper Ward
and State Apartments in Baroque Style.
Long Walk was laid out.*

CHARLES II

(1660 - 1685)

The Restoration of the monarchy was achieved on the King's 30th birthday following 8 years in exile. The Earl of Rochester commented that "he never said a foolish thing and never did a wise one".

Yet he could not forget the demise of his father Charles I when, during his own crowning ceremony on St George's Day 1661, he was officiated by the same Archbishop of Canterbury who had attended the Martyr King on the scaffold. In 1650 after being crowned by an act of Covenant King of Great Britain, France and Ireland he was forced to flee and hid in an oak tree, with a price of £100,000 on his head.

The Restoration of the monarchy was pro-

Dine in the house used by King Charles II, Church Street.

Windsor Castle, viewed from the Long Walk.

claimed in Windsor by the Mayor and Corporation "...with all joy acclamations", trumpets and drums playing. Windsor Castle became the King's summer residence and the principle palace outside London.

The architect Hugh May was charged with changing an "exceedingly ragged and ruinous" castle into a Baroque Palace. Remodelling of the State Apartments in the Upper Ward featured exquisite carvings in wood by Grinling Gibbons and huge ceiling decorations by the Italian painter Antonio Verrio. Sir Christopher Wren was appointed Surveyor General.

When the King held Court the atmosphere was pleasure seeking and marked by a languid sensuality. Verrio was appointed to decorate the stairway of the King's favourite mistress Nell Gwynn, mother of his son, the Duke of St. Albans.

Charles II created the long avenue of trees (Long Walk) being fond himself of walking as well as

impressing his contemporaries. In reverence to the ancient Order of the Knights of the Garter, St George's Chapel was restored from an internally ruinous state.

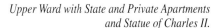

Upper Ward with State and Private Apartments and Statue of Charles II.

George III.

Initiated Gothic reconstruction of State Apartments.
Frogmore House was acquired.

GEORGE III

(1760 - 1820)

'Copper Horse', King George III's statue.

G eorge III purchased Buckingham House (now Palace) in 1762 for £21,000 yet favoured Windsor as a royal residence.

The King moved to Windsor in 1789 on recovering from his first illness of 'porphyria', referred to as the 'royal illness'. Two of his 15 children,

including his favourite Amelia, were born and died at Windsor.

In 1766 the Castle was described as "...the only place in England worthy to be styled a King's Palace (yet) so totally neglected". Queen Charlotte complained of the cold and draughts in the medieval Castle. Queen's Lodge was built to afford greater comfort, but later demolished by their son George IV who preferred an unimpeded view of the Long Walk. Today George III surveys his former Kingdom astride his mount, known as the 'Copper Horse'.

Windsor Castle, detail of Gothic reconstruction, State Apartment.

James Wyatt was appointed to Gothicize Charles II's Baroque additions. The present Grand Vestibule was a staircase in the late C18th, and retains the original elegant plaster fan-vaulted ceiling executed by Francis Bernasconi. George III's attraction for a lightened decorative appearance led to the oak wall panels in the King's Drawing Room being replaced with bright blue damask. What enlightened spirits the guests to the Queen's ballroom must have experienced, dancing beneath the finest examples of English glass chandeliers commissioned by George III. Frogmore House in Home Park was purchased. The King became known as 'Farmer George' because of his interest in Flemish and novel methods of farming.

The King's involvement with the trade and politics of the borough and familiarity with the townspeople earned him the nickname 'Squire of Windsor'. Fanny Burney, a famous novelist at the time wrote, "He knew something of the character and affairs of most persons who live under the shadow of the Castle". The public was rewarded by having regular access to the State Apartments of the Upper Ward and precincts. According to Miss Burney promenading on the South Terrace was popular since "...all Windsor and its neighbourhood poured in upon it, to see the prince" and the King who looked "so proud of his son". He spent the final years at Windsor Castle.

Peascod Street.

George IV.

Gothicized facade. Round Tower heightened.
Remodelling of State Apartments.
New Royal Apartments and Grand Corridor added.

GEORGE IV

(1820 - 1830)

Upper Ward showing Gothic pointed arched windows.

Windsor Castle, Round Tower.

The Duke of Wellington described him as "...the most extraordinary compound of talent, wit, buffoonery, obstinacy and good feelings".

While at banquets at the Castle he fancied himself having been present at the Battle of Waterloo. The Royal Collection at Windsor houses some of George IV's personal collection of finest china.

The King chose Jeffry Wyatville (nephew of James Wyatt) to continue the Gothic transformation of the Castle. His instructions were to "do everything in a substantial manner, and not merely vamp the building". The original estimate of £150,000 eventually exceeded £1 million.

Keen to improve the silhouette of the Castle, Henry II's Round Tower was raised by 33 feet. Extra towers and battlements were constructed. The knighted Sir Jeffry was said to have "....found a crumbling ruin and left the nation with a palace".

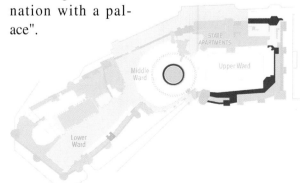

Waterloo Chamber.

King George IV took up residence in the Castle in 1828.

The King's fascination with the Battle of Waterloo led to the creation of the Waterloo Chamber, which commemorates the allied defeat of Napoleon. Measuring 180 feet (55 metres) in length, St George's Hall was created by Wyatville. Stepping into the Grand Reception Room is to experience the King's preference for C18th French panelling and gilded ornamentation. Formerly a ballroom, the Queen now meets her guests here as a prelude to State banquets. In the principal semi-state room, aptly named the Crimson Drawing Room, George IV was personally responsible for the choice of the rich crimson, silk damask wall covering (restored since the fire of 1992 and shown overleaf).

Queen Victoria.

Her Consort, Prince Albert, dies at Windsor.
Restoration Lower Ward.
Grand staircase to State Apartments rebuilt.

QUEEN VICTORIA

(1837 - 1901)

The 'Widow of Windsor' was the last Hanovarian sovereign. Herself the granddaughter of George III, four future sovereigns are related to Queen Victoria: Edward VII, George V, Edward VIII and George VI. In 1876 she became Queen-Empress of India.

At Windsor Castle, in the Blue Closet, she exercised a sovereign's prerogative and proposed marriage to her cousin, Albert of Saxe-Coburg-Gotha. The christening of her eldest son Edward (later Edward VII) took place within the splendour of St George's Chapel. Three of her children were married at the Castle. Queen Victoria chose to be buried in a mausoleum at Frogmore within the grounds of Windsor Park, and alongside her Consort Prince Albert, instead of in the royal Tombhouse constructed by George III.

During her reign the staterooms were used for entertaining Heads of State from around the World and Empire, including Napoleon III. The huge malachite urn in the Grand Reception Room was given by Tsar Nicholas I.

In 1851 Victoria's greatness was acknowledged by the Maharajah of Travancore's present of an Indian Ivory throne, which can now be marvelled at in the Queen's Grand Chamber. Queen Victoria still presides over the Grand Vestibule, her royal presence epitomised in marble by Joseph Boehm in 1871.

Queen Victoria's granite statue, erected in 1887, commemorates the 50th anniversary of her reign.

Queen Victoria arranged for Anthony Salvin to realign the Grand Staircase in 1866, for the sake of convenience. A Victorian addition is the conical roof to the Curfew Tower. A more personal remembrance of the Queen is the Albert Memorial Chapel. Situated to the east of St George's, the disused Wolsey Chapel was remodelled in marble and mosaic.

Statue of Queen Victoria and Windsor Castle.

Albert Memorial Chapel. Interior.

Lower Ward and Albert Memorial Chapel.

When Prince Albert died at the Castle on 14th December 1861, possibly of typhoid fever from unsafe drains, Victoria became a familiar figure dressed in mourning black. A virtual recluse, she no longer took tea occasionally with local commoners.

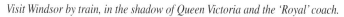

Visit Windsor by train, in the shadow of Queen Victoria and the 'Royal' coach.

Queen Elizabeth II.

Castle restored after serious fire damage.

QUEEN ELIZABETH II

(1952 -)

The Queen became Head of the Commonwealth in 1953. In 1977, during her Silver Jubilee year, she undertook a 56,000-mile tour of Commonwealth countries. Today the Queen plays a more strenuous role in the life of the nation than her predecessors.

Queen Elizabeth represents the House of Windsor. During the First World War King George V found it propitious to create the new Dynasty of Windsor, thereby affirming his allegiance of loyalty to the town and country.

During the Second World War the Princesses Elizabeth and Margaret were evacuated from London to Windsor along with more than 3,000 other children. To help keep up their spirits they joined with members of the royal household in performing pantomimes in the Castle's Waterloo Chamber. Two of their dolls, presented by the children of France in 1938, are on display in Queen Mary's Doll house. At Windsor the future Queen learned to drive a heavy lorry in aid of the war effort.

Five years before ascending the throne in 1952 the Queen was given the Honorary Freedom of the royal Borough of Windsor. Her Majesty responded "...I regard (Windsor) as home in a way no other

The Queen at Ascot Races.

place can be". Today the royal family regularly spend their private weekends at the Castle. While the Queen enjoys riding at the Royal Lodge, Prince Philip, a keen carriage driver, has competed in the internationally renowned Windsor Horse Show. His son, Prince Charles, became a familiar polo player at Smiths' Lawn while Princess Anne exhibited her equine skills at the cross-country horse trials in Windsor Great Park.

Every June the Garter Throne Room, with its carved and gilt throne canopy, witnesses the Queen's investiture of new Knights and Ladies of the Order of the Garter. Following the tradition of her ancestors, Queen Elizabeth holds ceremonial banquets for visiting Heads of State who may later find themselves sleeping in one of the reputedly capacious four-poster beds!

Windsor Castle, fire.

THE FIRE OF 1992

(P. 55) Windsor Castle, St George's Hall showing fire damage.

On the night of 20th November 1992 Windsor Castle was silhouetted against an inferno which began at 11am - raging for 15 hours and consuming 1/5th of the building. The initial spark ignited a curtain in the private chapel of the Upper Ward, spreading fire through the organ and into the roof space. Nine major state rooms were damaged, including the ancestral home of the Knights of the Garter, St George's Hall. Two hundred firemen fought the blaze using 1 1/2 million gallons of water. The Queen proclaimed 1992 her "annus horribilis".

Amazingly, only three items of major value were lost, including a Pugian sideboard which was too heavy to remove. In The Grand Reception Room the huge green malachite vase, given to Queen Victoria by Tsar Nicholas I, survived in situ. Bernasconi's elaborate plaster coving and gilded ceiling, though badly damaged, have been meticulously restored, thus once again encapsulating George IV's francophile taste. Original C17th crystalware remained completely intact in a serving room adjacent to the dining room.

THE RESTORATION

During the £40 million five-year restoration work of the Castle, Buckingham Palace was opened to the public to help finance the project. The restoration was carried out by 4000 British craftsmen. Portuguese tassels for the curtains were a fitting exception: the oldest treaty existing between Britain and another country is with Portugal and is called the treaty of Windsor! George IV's principal semi-state room, The Crimson Drawing Room, was restored to its former splendour and Wyatville's original hanging ceiling pinned to prevent the chandelier from swaying. Incredibly, a cardboard fan which had decorated the fireplace was untouched by the fire.

St George's Hall now boasts the largest oak hammerbeam roof to have been constructed in the C20th. Wyatville's flat plaster ceiling having collapsed, the new appearance is lighter and complements the heraldic decoration of shields representing every Garter Knight created. The redesigned private chapel of the Royal Family commemorates the fire of 1992 in a specially commissioned stained glass window. A new octagonal room, named the Lantern Lobby, was created on the site where the conflagration began. The exquisite inlaid floor of British marbles depicts the Garter Star. Reminiscent of Gothic columns and fan vaulting, the ceiling rises to a glazed lantern. The restoration was completed on the 50th anniversary of the wedding of Queen Elizabeth II and the Duke of Edinburgh. The Queen is said to have remarked that the restoration of Windsor Castle was the best anniversary present she could have wished for.

St George's Hall.

Crimson Room. Detail of restored ceiling.

Crimson Room. Detail of curtains with tassels.

WINDSOR BRIDGE

Windsor Bridge.

Cock Pit, Eton High Street.

The River Thames divides the towns of Windsor and Eton. Henry VIII and his spectacular cavalcade crossed here for the Castle in procession to celebrate the Garter Ceremony. Then the river was traversed by a wooden bridge. Today's cast-iron bridge, designed by Charles Hollis, was opened in 1850.

In gratitude to Joseph Taylor of Eton the bridge toll, allowed by Act of Parliament to recoup the great expense, was revoked in 1898.

Charles II is said to have frequented the 'Cock Pit' in Eton High Street which dates from Saxon times. In 1815 news of the Duke of Wellington's Victory at the Battle of Waterloo was first proclaimed in Eton.

Windsor Bridge viewed from the river.

ETON COLLEGE

Eton College is arguably the most well-known school in the world. Famous Etonians have included twenty Prime Ministers, the Duke of Wellington, George Orwell (author and political satirist) and Shelley, famous poet and husband of Mary Shelley who wrote the novel 'Frankenstein'. How would you recognise an Etonian by his uniform? In the late C18th the costume was described as consisting of "black cloaks or gowns, a square hat or cap.", still recognisable today!

Eton College.

Eton College Forecourt and Henry VI statue .

Henry VI laid the foundation stone in 1441. Etonians were intended to succeed to Oxford and Kings College Cambridge. On the anniversary of the King's death representatives of Eton and Kings College place white roses on his tomb in St George's Chapel. The King had made special provision for free schooling and accommodation for at least seventy underprivileged boys, from any part of the world. His original design of the chapel would have equalled that of St Paul's. During Henry VIII's reign, his apparent meanness was recorded. Although the College on one occasion spent £18 entertaining the King, Henry in return sought fit only to give 13s 14d to the church and £3 6s 8d for all the masters and pupils.

Eton College has survived the vicissitudes of time and the whims of monarchs. When Edward IV, temporarily ousted King Henry VI and became king in 1461, work on the college initially halted until William Westby, the Provost, persuaded the new King not to dissolve the institution. Neither the College nor the Provost however had the power to prevent the arrival of the Great Western railway in 1848, The Provost feared his boys would be corrupted by having speedy and easy access to London.

In March 1882, two Etonians helped to thwart the assassination attempt on Queen Victoria.

Traditional Eton College Outfitters.

Hampton Court Palace.

Hampton Court Palace, Clock Court.

HAMPTON COURT PALACE

S ituated beside the River Thames, Hampton Court Palace lies 13 miles upstream from London. This has been a royal residence since the C16th and the reign of King Henry VIII. Today the National Trust invites visitors on costumed guided tours to explore the treasures of our heritage.

Cardinal Wolsey, chief advisor and confidant for 16 years to the young King Henry VIII, leased the original Saxon manor for £50 per annum from the 'Knights Hospitallers'.

Great Kitchen.

Hampton Court Palace, Tudor Kitchens.

Hampton Court Palace comprises 1000 rooms, a Great Hall, Chapel and audience rooms all decorated with tapestries of gold and crimson thread and adorned with silver and gold plate, currently valued at £1 million. Living was made comfortable with silk upholstery and carpets brought from the East by Venetian merchants. At a cost of £50,000 clean water was piped from a spring 3 miles away. The 2000 acres of parkland were stocked with deer.

When, in June 1525, King Henry VIII asked Wolsey why he had built such a magnificent palace, the Cardinal was said to cleverly reply, "To show how noble a palace a subject may offer to his sovereign".

In spite of Wolsey having been described by a Venetian ambassador as "seven times greater than the Pope", he was obliged to transfer the lease of Hampton Court Palace to the King in an ill-fated attempt to retain the King's favour.

Henry's first wife, Catherine of Aragon, visited the palace during divorce proceedings in January 1529. Anne Boleyn spent her honeymoon here in 1533, pregnant with the future Queen Elizabeth I.

The Chapel was lavishly redecorated. Look skyward to the faithfully restored azure blue ceiling, the gold stars being a sentimental Victorian idea. Although little remains of Henry's apartments, Jane Seymour and the beheaded 5th wife, Catherine Howard, are said to haunt the Queen's Apartments and Upper Gallery. At Hampton Court the future King Edward VI, Henry's only legitimate surviving male heir, was born on 12th October 1537. Jane, Henry's favourite wife, died 12 days later following his birth.

When walking through the Great Kitchen imagine the smells and tastes of the adjacent bakeries, sauceries, meat and poultry kitchens and wine cellar. Children turned the spits carrying whole wild boar and deer.

A larger Great Hall was erected measuring 160' long, 40' wide and 60'high.

Hampton Court Palace, Wine Cellar.

For entertainment, Henry introduced indoor tennis from France. In the parterre garden of formal hedges Henry courted Catherine Howard, immediately following his divorce from the 4th wife, Anne of Cleves.

Mary Tudor honeymooned at the Palace with her groom Philip II of Spain. Princess Elizabeth was held in custody by Mary, returning as Queen to the Palace for rest and quiet, working in the gardens for 1 hour each morning. Exotic plants were brought from abroad by Raleigh and Hawkins. William Shakespeare performed plays here. The eligible Elizabeth received marriage proposals and plans at the Palace, but rejected them all.

Queen Elizabeth's successor, King James I of England and Scotland, hosted the conference of the so-called "Millenary Petition" in 1604: Puritan demand for simplified religious observance.

During the Civil War King Charles II was impris-

Hampton Court Palace and Privy Gardens.

Sir Christopher Wren was commissioned by King William III to build a rival to Louis XIV's palace at Versailles. Rectangular massive structures redolent of the French Renaissance replaced most of the Tudor haphazard skyline. Antonio Verrio's painted ceiling and walls still adorn the King's Grand Staircase.

George II and Queen Caroline were the last two British Sovereigns to actually live in the Palace. The grounds were further reshaped by the later famous 'Capability Brown'.

William IV restored Hampton Court to its former glory. Unfortunately, on Easter Monday 1986, fire destroyed much of the south range of Wren's Fountain Court. A policy of 'total salvage' restored 75 per cent of the original oak panelling and 64 per cent of the original mouldings.

Hampton Court Palace Parterre Garden.

oned at the Palace, escaping via a private passage to the Water Gallery (where princess Elizabeth had previously been imprisoned).

Following the King's execution, Oliver Cromwell, Lord Protector of the Commonwealth, lived here simply and economically.

When Charles II acceded to the throne in 1660 Louis XIV's landscape gardener was borrowed to restructure the formerly flat parkland.

Hampton Court Palace, Fountain Court.

LEGOLAND

Legoland, main entrance.

The domain of Legoland beckons within a short journey from Windsor.

At Legoland, children of all ages from grandchildren to grandparents can be creative, have fun, develop the imagination, play and learn in an exciting yet safe environment. Learn to drive a Duplo car or sail in a make-believe harbour. Create your own robot and learn to control a

sophisticated computer. Allow your imagination free reign while exploring Miniland with its scaled replica of famous London sights. The Dragon Knight's Ride and Pirate Falls offer excitement for the more daring visitor. Legoland also caters for those who seek a few moments of quietude and relaxation in the Enchanted Forest.

Legoland is full of surprises. Aerial circus acts vie for your attention with spectacular stunt displays. Throughout the year, special events are held. On the morning of New Year's Eve 2000, Legoland celebrated the arrival of the new Millenium as it took place in Australia. Why not celebrate your own special event, such as a birthday, at Legoland?

Need to give that imagination of yours a rest or just ravenous? The Park has a number of eating places which cater for all tastes and pockets.

Legoland, the Dragon Ride.

Legoland, Tower Bridge.

The Splendour of
WINDSOR
ETON, HAMPTON COURT AND LEGOLAND

Graphics: Storti Edizioni S.r.l.

Photography:
Powel Libera

Text: Danuta Balcerowska
BA (HON.) London University

THOMAS BENACCI LTD
Unit 21 Bessemer Park
250 Milkwood Road
Herne Hill - London SE24 OHG
Tel. 207-9240635
Fax 207-9240636
e-mail: nelrom@aol.com
www.thomasbenacci.co.uk

The Publisher wishes to thank photographers and all the institutions, museums and galleries listed below for their kind permission to reproduce photographs in this book.

• *'The Royal Collection © 2000, Her Majesty Queen Elizabeth II':*
  pages 19 - 30/31 - 51 John Freeman; page 47; pages 48/49 - 56 - 57 Mark Fiennes.
• *'The National Portrait Gallery London':*
  pages 20 - 22 - 23 - 24 - 26 - 32 - 36 - 38 - 40 - 42 - 44 - 46 - 50 - 52 - 53.
• *Ag.Grazia Neri: page 30.*
• *Air Picture page 2/3 The SKYSCAN Photo Library.*
• *David Levenson / Colorific: page 54*
• *Legoland: page 63*

CONTENTS

Plan of Windsor and Eton 4
Town Walkabout 6
Entertainment....................................... 9
River Thames 11
The Long Walk and 'Copper Horse' 13
Windsor Castle 14
Plan of the Castle 18
William the 'Conqueror' 20
Henry II 22
Henry III 23
Edward III 24
Edward IV 26
St George's Chapel.................................. 28
Henry VIII 32
Queen Mary I 36
Elizabeth I 38
Charles I 40
Charles II 42
George III 44
George IV 46
Queen Victoria 50
Queen Elizabeth II 52
The Fire of 1992 54
The Restoration 56
Windsor Bridge 58
Eton College 59
Hampton Court Palace 60
Legoland 63

Cover:
Round Tower on William I's Motte viewed from river.